Search high and low
Memory Maker

Complete Today's Point

Find the matching letters and fill in the sentence.

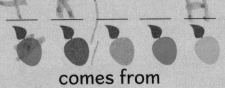

___ ___ ___ ___ ___

comes from

___ ___ ___

Satan Tricked Adam and Eve

Genesis 2–3

God created Adam and Eve and placed them in the garden of Eden. God told them they could not eat from the tree of knowing good and bad. Satan pretended to be a snake and tried to trick them. He wanted Adam and Eve to choose to do what they wanted to do instead of obeying God. Adam and Eve chose to eat the fruit. Adam and Eve then knew about good and bad. Their choice was against God's plan for them. God told them about the bad things that would happen because of their choice. God said that one day He would send a man to beat (win against) Satan. God sent Jesus. Jesus told people that God loves them and wants to forgive them.

What's Different?

Look at the pictures and circle what is different. See if you can find all five differences!

Daniel Chose God's Way

Daniel 1

Daniel and his friends were captured by King Nebuchadnezzar of Babylon. The king ordered that the young men who had been captured should be served the king's food and drink and be trained for three years. Then they would serve the king. Daniel asked if he and his friends could eat only vegetables and drink water. He wanted to follow God's plan with the foods he ate. Daniel and his friends were healthier and stronger than all the other men who had been eating the king's food! The friends chose to follow God's plan. The king found the four friends were the best of all the men who had been working for him.

Trace the tail of each kite to the sandy shore to find each day's Point from this week.

Day 1
Truth comes from God.

Day 2
God's plan is best.

Day 3
Everyone needs Jesus.

Day 4
The Bible is true!

Day 5
Speak the truth in love.

Design a quilt to take to the beach. Use the instructions below.

- Use green on the squares where you see a tree.
- Use orange on the squares where you see a pitcher and bowl.
- Use blue on the squares where you see a coin bag.
- Use purple on the squares where you see a cross.
- Use red on the squares where you see a heart.
- Choose your favorite colors for the remaining squares.

Tell a friend something from the Bible stories these pictures remind you of.

The Rich Young Ruler

Mark 10:17-27

Jesus is the One God promised would come to fix the relationship between God and people. One day a rich man asked Jesus how to get to heaven. Jesus reminded the man of God's rules. The man said he had followed those rules. Jesus told the man to sell all his things and follow Jesus. The rich man went away sad. A person does not have to sell everything to get to heaven, but the rich man cared more about his things than following Jesus. One of God's rules is that we should love Him more than anything. God wants us to live in heaven with Him someday. God sent His Son, Jesus, because He loves us. We should love Jesus more than anything.

Count the Coins

Draw a line from each coin in the box to the number of coins you find on the pages.

5

3

9

2

6

7

4

8

Trace the Lines

Trace the lines and finish designing
your beach towel.

John Wrote about Jesus

John 14:1-6; 18—20; Acts 1:9-12

One night when they were all together, Jesus ate with the disciples (helpers). Jesus talked about things that were going to happen, and then He went to a garden to pray. Soldiers arrested Jesus even though He hadn't done anything wrong. Jesus died on a cross, and His body was placed in a tomb. Three days later, Jesus was alive again! Jesus talked and even ate with John and the other disciples (helpers). Many days later, John saw Jesus return to heaven on a cloud. John wrote about these things in one of his books in the Bible. He said everything he wrote was true. He saw it happen.

Complete the Pattern

Draw a line from the item that completes the pattern to the box where it belongs.

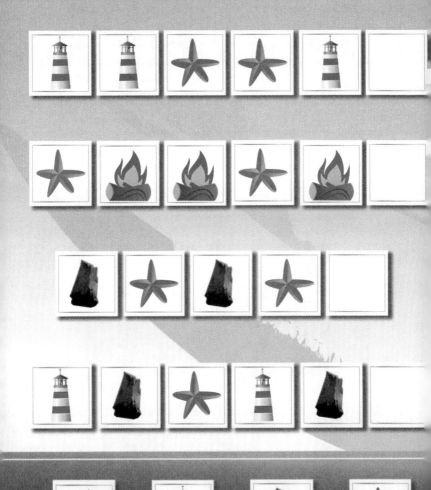

Paul Encouraged the Ephesians

Acts 9:1-6; 19:1-10,21-31; 20:1; Ephesians 3:14—4:16

After Paul started following Jesus, he told people about Jesus wherever he went. Paul visited a town named Ephesus. God did amazing things there. Many people became followers of Jesus, but some people started saying bad things about Paul and started a fight in the city. Later Paul wrote a letter to the church at Ephesus. Paul knew what life was like there. Followers of Jesus were made fun of and treated badly. Paul reminded the people that God loved them. He said they should show God's love to others whether they agreed with them or not. Paul told the people to grow and learn more about Jesus so they would know God's truth and not be easily tricked. He told the followers to always speak God's truth with love.

Open the Bible

Open your Bible to the book listed and then
color the circle around the Daily Icon! Ask a parent, teacher,
or friend if you would like help.

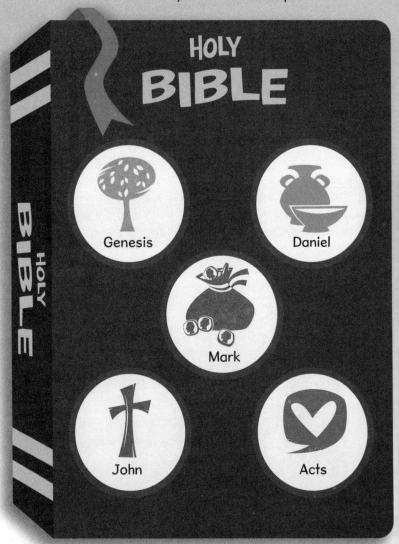

HOLY
BIBLE

Genesis

Daniel

Mark

John

Acts